I0109070

BRANCHING IN:

THE JOURNEY FROM ALONE TO ALL ONE

Dieter and Jenny Randolph

Copyright © 2016 Dieter and Jenny Randolph

Published by Unity Society, LLC

http://unitysociety.com

All rights reserved.

ISBN: 0692816607
ISBN-13: 978-0692816608

For Miles and Raina

CONTENTS

ACKNOWLEDGEMENTS

Most of this book was written on the morning walks we take by the water and through downtown Saint Petersburg, Florida. There are a number of characters we've met along the way, and seen almost every morning, who have each done their part to inspire us. We'll use the nicknames here; you know who you are. Special thanks to Ray Ray, the Duct Tape Walker, the Guru, the Electric Company, the Bench Watcher, Festival Staff, and the Mayor of the Volleyball Court. This book would not have happened without all the people who stopped to share a sunrise or a dolphin spotting with us. No matter where we walk, we always end up at Kahwa Coffee -- we are eternally grateful for the endless half-caf coconut milk lattes from the world's finest (and nicest) baristas.

We're also grateful for the love, support, and inspiration provided by some amazing Unity ministers, including Andy Conyer, Jennifer Sacks, Elizabeth Thompson, Cynthia Alice Anderson, Nancy Norman, and, most of all, Temple Hayes. Reverend Temple and the First Unity community have changed our lives, and they are changing the world.

We'd like to express our gratitude to the current and former members of the Youth of Unity. We were YOUers when we met, and we like to think that we carry some of that spirit with us today. We know that the future is in good hands, and we're grateful for the light that you are. We've worked with some amazing sponsors, including Mitch, Alex, Amy, and Andrew. Thank you for your loyalty and steadfast friendship.

Most of all, we want to thank you for joining us on this ongoing journey. Thanks for being part of the revolution.

FOREWORD: A NOTE FROM MILES AND RAINA RANDOLPH

Mom is a child of seekers. Her parents brought her along on their generation's quest for peace and enlightenment. She's been Mormon, Buddhist, SRF, Baptist, and just about everything else. She tells a great story about speaking in tongues at an Assemblies of God meeting, and another about her Transcendental Meditation teacher falling asleep during a session. Dad is a preacher's kid, like us. His parents and grandparents were Unity ministers.

Our parents come from different places, but they're always on the same page. From an early age, they each learned the importance of work. Then, and now, that's what people think of when they think of Mom and Dad. They work, and things happen. As we hear their stories we know they were looking for answers. More than that, they were looking for each other.

They met in church.   They were both in their teens when they crossed paths in a Youth of Unity classroom. As corny as it sounds, they knew in that moment that they'd reached the end of one journey and started a new one. Their first conversation was more of an argument; about what *Lessons in Truth's* author was trying to say.   But that's them.   Their story, up until that moment, had been independent study. After that day it was a collaborative effort. Along with the "normal" teenage concerns, our parents dedicated themselves to growth in a way that continues to inspire us. Their extracurricular activity list was like something out of folklore. Some people stop trying once they meet their life partner, but these two seemed to kick into high gear. Maybe that's how you know when you've met your soulmate; you want to try harder and do more.

1994 was a big year for them. They'd been together for a while, and decided to take the next step and get engaged. As always, a public declaration of "we mean it" brings an answer from the universe. In that one year, Mom graduated from high school, Dad became a minister, they got married, started a storefront church, and became parents. There were many milestones in that 365 days, but the tempo is the same every year. A lot of things have changed in the decades that they've spent together, but it's never been anything but intense.

Passion is important in our house. Instead of sending us to school, our parents asked us what inspired us, and made it educational. As our interests changed, the curriculum evolved. The overall lesson stayed the same: Life is an educational event, so there isn't any boundary between learning and living. As long as you are faithful to your heart's calling, you'll grow.

Whether you know it or not, your calling is calling you. Mom can't go to the grocery store without being stopped by a total stranger who wants advice. When our family was just starting out, Dad took on any extra work he could find. Wherever he went, whether he was in a cubicle or a used car lot, people sought him out to talk about deep questions and spiritual answers.

Everybody has a calling. Everybody has a role to play in the demonstration of Spirit. For some people, that heart's desire is buried under low self-esteem, personality issues, and guilt. The calling still calls. Sooner or later we all learn how to listen. When we connect inner desire with conscious thought and then loving action, things happen. We grow, and we encourage others to do the same. That's how you know you're on the right track. When an idea gets so big that you can't keep quiet about it, but instead have to share it with others, you're on your way. The goal is inspiration, for ourselves and others.

You are holding an "un-book." The fundamental idea here is that you already have what it takes. This book is unique, because you're not going to read that you're doing or thinking something wrong. Instead, the goal is to bring out something *right* that's already there. We all take part in the same story, so of course we're going to talk about some things you already know. It may be that this is the validation and accountability you need to move beyond your current pattern. Start where you are, honoring the facts and the Truth of your situation, and you'll grow from there. With that attitude, lessons are everywhere.

There are no secret teachings here. This is important to know; some people start a journey like this with the goal of uncovering something hidden. We can't tell you how many times people have come to our parents asking for the spiritual equivalent of a password or a secret handshake. We don't believe that this path should have trade secrets, because we're talking about something that is inherently known and explicitly demonstrated. There is no key to the clubhouse here, but the good news is that it's unlocked.

A while ago we were helping our parents chaperone an overnight church event for teens. As always, it was a lot of fun working with them. We had just finished settling in for the night and all the kids were finally in their beds. We started talking about the day, and laughing at some of the teenage drama that usually accompanies these types of weekends. We also talked about how to break through with some of them and hoped that they would see the bigger picture of life and focus on more than the superficial.

Being a teenager feels like being at sea. We talked about what it means to be on a boat, sailing on the waters of unexpressed potential. Everybody has choices about where that journey will take them, whether or not to be afraid, and even what it might mean to feel spiritually seasick. We are here to fish, to set our line, cast it into those waters, and then trust the process. Some people fixate on cutting bait. Others spend all their time dreaming about a big catch and miss nibbles along the way.

Spiritual seekers tend to be good at prep work. There are always more books, workshops, and techniques to learn, and they're all wonderful. A full bookshelf doesn't guarantee a full life. The trick is in conscious application of what we've learned. The goal isn't anything esoteric. It's about being good at fishing, in the metaphor as well as in the example set by Jesus and the disciples. The goal is being good at life, and that means knowing the teachings, but also doing something about them. It means letting go, too.

Most people would be happy to drift off to sleep and maybe gossip a little bit about the kids. Mom and Dad turned that moment into a life-changing parable. This is what it's like living in our family. This book is a snapshot of life in our house. It started with the fishing story, and evolved through the morning walks that our parents take. It became clear that they were on to something, and they decided to test that feeling by teaching a class based on that ongoing conversation. It was amazing to sit in those classes with so many other people who were getting excited about the things we hear around the dinner table every night. From there, the feedback and insights from the class were incorporated into the project. The next step took the form of blog posts on unitysociety.com. I think we're all surprised at how popular the site has become. It's so much fun to know that these old ideas are resonating with a new audience.

You are holding the latest step in this evolutionary journey. You're the key to what happens next. Thanks for coming along.

INTRODUCTION

Everybody wants to connect. Each person has a desire for an experience of transcendence, love, or a bigger life. Some call that pull evolution, and for some it's a matter of spiritual development. What if it's both?

We share this fundamental calling with every living thing. We aren't any different from the elephants, the salmon, the turtles, or any of the countless species that are programmed to return to source. This is a more complicated process for humans. Our basic drives are not just instinctual. They are instead filtered through past experience, present judgement, and future expectation.

Our beautiful variety of interpretation has led to a wide range of attempts to address the primal calling. History is full of examples of the ways in which we have dealt with the challenge of existence. The challenge itself is expressed variously. In essence, it's this: we all crave permanence and Truth, but the material world is in constant flux.

The response to this dynamic has often involved a little bit of willful ignorance. Some people choose to avoid any kind of transcendent experience or ultimate concern, and instead seek fulfillment in materialism. This means being blind to the inherently transient nature of the world around us. On the other end of the spectrum, some people reject materiality completely, and spend their lives seeking spiritual escape. To do this necessitates an abandonment of any hope that the current situation might be good, educational, or worthy of attention.

Either way, half of the experience is set aside, and so either way, there's a fair bit of frustration to deal with. It is the nature of material things to change, to wear out, to prove entropy. Looking for stability and fulfillment in the fundamentally temporal is a recipe for heartbreak. While Spirit does not take part in thermodynamics, a willful rejection of the present moment prevents us from being happy right now, much less getting where we want to go. There's another option. Here's our position:

It's all good.

We're using this book to suggest a different approach. Instead of throwing away what you already know, we are hoping you can bring it to the discussion. We are not going to tell you that you're wrong, that your experience and your feelings are bad, or that succeeding in one area means leaving the others behind. Instead, we want you to love everything about where you are so that you can move on to something even better. The way to embrace the challenge of existence is to see your present material circumstances as finite examples of an infinite nature. Bless them for what they are rather than trying to make them into what they are not.

When you look closely enough, every created thing bears the fingerprints of its creator. No matter what's going on in life, the decision to see it as evidence of something bigger unlocks a spiritual connection and unlimited potential. We call this exercise "Branching In," because we are working from many individual manifestations to one timeless Truth. There is a great deal of pressure to diffuse our attentions and energies, to solve our problems by adding more opinions and techniques to our lives. But if you are inherently good, healing is not an additive process. You don't need anything extra to be who you already are. Branching In is the process of understanding the current moment as the fruit of a more profound life experience. We follow it through branch and trunk back to root, and use that expanded awareness as the seed of something new.

We are not writing this to instruct you as much as to remind you. Your True nature is pure, beautiful, and unstoppable. That real self shines through your present moment. The more you remember who you are, and the more you live with authenticity, the better your experience becomes. Along the way, what's happening right now can tell you what you need to know.

There are no accidents. You are in this life to learn and teach, to love and be loved, to liberate and celebrate. Growth can't happen when we curse the profound or the superficial parts of life. Instead, the goal is to look through the facts and into the Truth.

The key to success, prosperity, and freedom is to bless and praise what's happening right here and now. It is a momentary example of the eternal.

This middle path is the way to embrace our fundamental calling, our primal nature. We didn't paint on cave walls because we wanted to reject the immanent or deny the transcendent. We did it because we wanted to connect the present and the permanent, the material and the divine. This is the real motivation behind every human action; it's the reason we fall in love. We wrote this book to help you fall in love with your life.

We've been on this path for a long time. We know that this kind of life takes work and more than a little trust. There have been plenty of times when we weren't sure how things would work out for our family, but we were able to move forward in faith. Sometimes that process was effortless, and answers revealed themselves beautifully. Sometimes things felt so tough that we had no choice but to give up conscious control and let Spirit be in charge. That was beautiful, too. Both of those kinds of experiences are blessings, and both confirm the concept that life is good, even when there's a temptation to call things bad.

Something interesting happened in those "bad" times. We believe that what we hold in consciousness is what we experience in life; that our world is the result of our thoughts, words, and actions. Every moment proves this to be the case. It's not too hard to take that empowering concept and turn it into something negative, though. If life isn't working, if things feel bad, it's not hard to decide that it means that you are bad, too, that there's something wrong. Every thought creates. Thoughts of negativity and blame don't bring a happy next experience. And then we have a pretty unpleasant spiral. Eventually it's not hard to start believing that the whole world is broken.

That's a choice, of course. The moment we change our minds, the moment we agree with a good idea, the manifestation changes too. The spiral starts going in the other direction. Let's choose to believe that existence doesn't always have to go along with our plans, and that Spirit has a better idea. Let's decide that every moment of the wonderful messiness of life is conspiring to help us grow. That means honoring the good feelings and the bad ones; it means denying denial.

The process we're going to work through in this book is one you have already experienced: See, Speak, and Surrender. Start with a vision, take it into action, and then let it go. This is a universal recipe. These are the steps farmers live by, for example. They learn about the planting process and choose what seeds they want, then plant those seeds and water them. They then let them grow in their own time. All three steps are necessary to the process. This is the key to every successful effort in life. It's also everywhere in Scripture. One example is Matthew 21:21, where we read "If you have faith and do not doubt, you can say to the mountain 'be up and cast into the sea,' and it will be done for you." The faith comes first, then the action, and then we get out of the way and it is done *for* us. A lot of people are good at one or two steps, but success requires all three.

Some people think that spirituality starts with the middle part, and spend all their time finding the "correct" words or rituals. Without the right vision and intention, without faith, nothing we do matters. Some people are good at holding the vision, but never do anything about it. Some people live in a state of surrender, with mixed results at best. Right here and now, please take a moment to think about which parts of this process you specialize in. Think about which parts could use more attention.

See, Speak, and Surrender is a great pattern for life, and it's the pattern this book will take. Each chapter starts with a summary that outlines its focus in light of the process, so you'll know what to look for and work on. Each chapter ends with question helps designed to take the principles out of your head and into your experience.

This is a workbook. We hope that reading it makes you feel good, but that feeling is not the goal. Instead, happiness is a byproduct, a signpost. When we feel good, life is trying to tell us that we're on the right path, but that does not mean that the journey is over. We still have walking, and working, to do.

You may have good days and bad days. You may have times when you go from success to success. You may have times when the universe asks you if you mean what you say. Either way, you're allowed to feel your feelings. Celebrate the spectrum of experiences. Live the fullest, messiest, most beautiful version of your life that you can. Your current feelings tell you where you're at, and that information will help you get where you want to go.

Embrace the moment as a growth opportunity, and you'll grow.

We want to work with you. We don't want the book you are holding to feel like an external authority or a set of rules to memorize. Instead, we want you to be part of an ongoing discussion. When we taught Branching In in the classroom, the process felt natural and organic. We decided to write this book in a dialogue format to preserve that feeling. The most important part of this journey is what you bring to it.

CHAPTER ONE: THE FORMULA

Whether we are conscious of them or not, our beliefs define our experience. Our fundamental worldview, the formula we use to define ourselves and interact with life, is where our journey starts. We can only have a life as good as the standards we set and accept for ourselves. The key to growth is conscious involvement. Set your expectations deliberately, and you can live on purpose.

SEE:

Realize that the rules you live by set the standard for your experience; they help or limit based on how closely they reflect the Truth.

SPEAK:

You have the right to choose aspirational ways of living and thinking. Choose how you'd like to grow, and decide what thoughts, words, and actions can get you there in healthy ways.

SURRENDER:

Acknowledge that your identity affects your authenticity, and trust the process.

JENNY:

I want to talk about engagement. I think that it's a part of the process that gets taken for granted. People can read and study and have all kinds of information, but never do anything with what they've got. I think that it's fun to prepare for a journey, but until we embark there's not much point. How can we move forward if we never actually do anything with our ideas? If we are thinking in terms of ultimate oneness, if we don't have room in our cosmology for duality, then there also isn't room for "before," "during," or "after" the spiritual path. You and I and everyone else are already on it.

Along the way we establish a set of rules and expectations that we live by. Some of them come from society and upbringing, some come from work and life, and some come from learning the hard way. For most people, the rules are unspoken and largely unexamined.

It's time for an awakening. Consciousness is power; it takes us out of have-to and into want-to. I think it would be empowering to stop talking about cramming for life's exam, and instead start asking how we are enjoying the trip.

DIETER:

I love that. For one thing, it gets people to a place where they acknowledge that they are already on the road and part of this process. Like it or not. There's something powerful about conscious involvement. Being aware that you are in process is the beginning to making healthy changes. There aren't any wrong answers; it's a great thing to be working on life at all. In a way, no matter what process a person is using, they can't be wrong. I say that for a few reasons. For one thing, wherever we are we have the potential for growth, so there's no "bad" option. Whether we learn the easy way or the hard way, we all learn.

Every system works, up to a point. Think about how many times we've had somebody tell us about the latest self-help, or diet, or pop spirituality book.

It's perpetual. There are some great books out there, but on one level it doesn't even matter if they're particularly good or even novel. Every diet book, for example, will help you lose a few pounds, because it can act as a MacGuffin. I love that word -- *MacGuffin* is a movie nerd word; an Alfred Hitchcock word. It means a thing that drives the plot of a movie forward, but we as viewers don't have to care about it. There are all kinds of examples, from the statue in The Maltese Falcon and the suitcase in Pulp Fiction to the diamond necklace in Titanic. In all those examples, the quest for the object is what it takes to get all the characters moving, but that's it. After about ten minutes we can stop worrying about whether it gets found, who gets it, or even what it is.

Sometimes we just need a MacGuffin to get started. Any book, or workshop, or guru can kickstart a healing process. With a little attention and intention, and with the basic assertion that you are capable of and worth growth, you can make progress. But that only goes so far, because when you place your power outside of yourself, you can't reach the real goal, which is self-empowerment. That's why there's always a sequel, a new book, an improved process. The problem isn't in the material, it's in the underlying idea that something external can fix us. For one thing, we aren't ever any more broken than we decide to be. If you believe that there is something so wrong with you that you need something alien, you won't grow past a certain point.

Life can feel so overwhelming. There's a temptation to settle for surviving, when thriving is what we want and need. A commodity-based notion of growth might get you started. It might help you find a place of safety, but it can't get you where you need to go. In fact, a lot of times the cycle is like what we might see in addiction. There's always a bigger fix required because nothing external can fill an internal hole.

JENNY:

And it is a cycle -- so often there are repeating elements. Let's discuss what all self help books, diets and general "get better" systems have in common. It seems like they all follow the same formula. I think the first thing that has to be there in order for them to sell it to you is that you have to be wrong. They all start out saying that you aren't quite good enough. It's not always obvious but the sentiment is always there. You might be eating the wrong food, saying the wrong words, or living in the wrong part of the world. There's an endless list of how we're living our lives the wrong way. Think about it. You are routinely asked to give up something. You are routinely told that your thoughts and actions are all wrong and you should change. You are routinely given the message that you are not enough. TV ads do this all the time. One of the most common psychology tricks you see in commercials is connecting a feeling of error with something we take for granted. For example, there's an ad I see all the time for a haircare product. At the beginning, the narrator tells us that every time we wash our hair with normal shampoo we are doing all kinds of damage. Now when I wash my hair, it's hard not to think of that commercial and the "harm" I'm doing. The commercial wins by making me feel wrong, and furthermore by telling me that the only way to get back to right is through its product. There is an art to creating artificial necessity. The process feeds a lot of what happens in economics, culture, and life. We have so much technology, so many cures and solutions. But I bet modern people experience the sensation of *need* just as much, if not more, than members of so-called "primitive" cultures. The slippery slope happens when we accept the proposition that our answer is outside of us. That paradigm creates a hole that can't be filled. As long as you believe you are fundamentally erroneous, no external answers are good enough.

DIETER:

You start out being wrong. And if you are wrong, what you need is some kind of sage or ninja master to guide you. You can't do it on your own. And for some reason the guru is more interesting or trustworthy if they come from somewhere else. It's not that the guy down the block, the guy just like me, has some insights that might help. It's always somebody from a faraway land who has nothing in common with me and my wrongness. Sometimes it's a long-dead master speaking from the beyond or something. I can't help but feel like the attraction has less to do with what the teacher is saying and more to do with the fact that it's broadcast from a distance. It's like a personification of the old geographical cure idea. And it gets under my skin for all the same reasons. The grass isn't any holier on the other side. Location doesn't guarantee wisdom. When somebody would ask him about some ascended master or guide from "the other side," my dad would say "what makes somebody smart, just because they're dead?"

JENNY:

Now fast forward. Let's say that you've been following a certain method for a while. You have given your power away and have made the decision that the gurus are right and you're wrong. But because your good is coming not from inside you but from something external it's not sustainable. Sooner or later you are going to fall short. If you are eating nothing but kale smoothies, at some point you're going to break down and have a french fry and milkshake party. The problem now is that because you couldn't live up to some imaginary standard, the guilt and blame start to creep in. It *must* be you because look at all the other people who were able to succeed. It really is a vicious cycle.

DIETER:

Even though everybody else is thinking the same thing. But with that feeling of shared alienation people build an imaginary world. Where I am isn't great, but when I live in this dream world prescribed by the method I'm trying to follow, that's better somehow. There is often an element of world denial; the idea there seems to be that the goal of the system is to escape. I'm supposed to pack my spiritual bags and get away. The masters of these systems are from a faraway place. My situation, right here and now, is something to flee from. We see this a lot in the spiritual end of things, but it applies universally. The gotcha there is that if I'm always trying to escape, it's hard to make a positive difference where I am. Can you imagine being in a romantic relationship with somebody but telling them "I'm only with you until the right person comes along?" It's not healthy or sustainable, but that's the kind of relationship folks can have with the world around them if they're not careful.

JENNY:

I think there is also an element of *self*-denial. There's this theory that your feelings and instincts are wrong. If you can't fit in or follow the rules, it's not the system, it's your ideas that are bad. We're told to suppress our natural instincts and to ignore when something isn't working. We're told if we just work hard enough or suffer long enough we'll get to where we want to be. If we get mad or sad in the process there must be something wrong with us.

We are in this human experience. To have a fully expressed life, we will have times when negative emotions are going to happen. But that doesn't make you wrong. In fact it's a little bit strange to ignore something as basic as emotions or instincts. Don't we tell our children to trust their guts in strange situations? When we take a test we're told to answer with our first impulse. Why are we not following our own suggestions? When we hear the phrase "follow your heart," or any one of a million variations of that sentiment, our hearts sing.   We know it's the Truth.

THE OLD FORMULA:

- You are Wrong
- Distant Authority
- Reliance on Method
- World Denial
- Self Denial

DIETER:

People might see this formula at work at their church, and so they stop going. I do think it's healthy to ask for better answers, but there are a couple of problems there. First of all, it's a leap to decide that *all* religions are bad; that's a baby and bathwater situation. It's a little like deciding that all restaurants are bad because some of them serve junk food.

Many times people walk away from a church but unconsciously apply that same formula to their job, or relationship, or spirituality.   We have a need to gather and work through issues of ultimate concern. That's all religion is, anyway. Spirituality is about how you feel, and religion is about what you do. And we all want to do something; it's what we're built for. Giving up on action and staying in receive-only mode might be tempting, but it's not helpful. So for a lot of folks the itch remains, unscratched.

JENNY:

I think it's important to acknowledge that we are social creatures. On a biological level as well as spiritual. There's a reason that we gather together for sporting events. There's a reason that we go and pay a small fortune to see the latest Star Wars movie with a group of like-minded people. We get more pleasure out of it when we come together and have a shared experience. There is a sense of community. A sense that we're not alone. And church is no different. There's something beautiful about gathering together to share spiritual ideas and rituals.

I think it's also important to remember that nobody does anything alone. Unlike most animals, humans are helpless at birth. We care for each other from that point forward. Every success story you've ever heard has a huge supporting cast. Somebody gave the hero their first break. They taught them something fundamental, or sparked an idea. They encouraged that person to keep growing.

DIETER:

And we are hard-wired to grow. Spiritually, biologically, and in every other way the basic nature of each of us is evolution. It's table stakes. No matter what else you have going on, where you've been or what you see for the future, the Truth about you is growth. It is the motivating factor behind everything we do.

By the way, if you're having a hard time with somebody, one way to find some common ground is to remember that they're here to grow, just like you are. Their ideas about how to grow and in which direction might need some TLC, but the pull is the same. In fact, letting people evolve by their own standard is important, because we need that for ourselves, too. Just as you've said, it's our nature to want to grow with other people, in the context of community. The problem is when our measuring stick is outside ourselves.

JENNY:

Exactly. Maybe we learn to give our power away or to compete with other people, which amounts to the same thing. And when we are small, maybe it's healthy to have external sanctions. But we grow up. Living with the belief that other people have something we want, and that we have no access to the source of good in our lives, isn't healthy. It causes transactional relationships. It's commodity-based, where the only reason we are with somebody is because of something they give us, instead of something we experience and work through together. And that leads to blame. If we make somebody else our God, so to speak, and we don't like where our lives are, it makes a certain kind of sense that we'd see it as their fault.

If we are only good because we want to provoke a reaction in somebody else, we're not doing things for the right reasons. Do kids go to school because they want to get a good education, or do they go with the idea that if they sit still for a few hours they'll get to go home? Do you drive safe because it's a virtue, or because you know you might get a ticket otherwise? These experiences, and a million others, happen when power is given away, and they feel wrong because that's exactly what they are.

DIETER:

The biggest problem with external validation is that there's a tendency to experience a feeling of victory in the failures of others. If I think there's not enough good to go around, I'm bound to feel like most of it is somewhere else. If I really believe that, I'm bound to feel like a winner when somebody else loses.   Naturally, that kind of thinking ends up holding everybody back.   Growth is a matter of increasing the amount of good experienced overall, not by keeping it the same and just shifting it around. This is a great self-test.   Do you catch yourself cheering when somebody else falls?   That's a good indicator that you have some limiting thoughts rolling around in there.

JENNY:

The irony is that people start this journey with that natural desire to unify with others. But doing it in this way, seeking external validation, ends up being the most divisive thing of all. What if instead of starting from outside we started with what we have on the inside? What if good isn't something we get but something we bring? There is enough good to go around.   Instead of blaming we can inspire. Instead of competing we can share.

DIETER:

Start with the knowing that you already have what it takes to grow. That's just the deal. If I throw a ball to you, you'll catch it. It doesn't take much, and it's completely natural. When you think about it, though, there's a lot going on there. The math and physics involved in charting the ball's path, the biology and physiology in what my arm is doing, and so on. There are encyclopedias worth of information happening in that little interaction. I can go get PhDs in the various fields involved, and that might help, but at the end of the day there's nothing like just catching the ball when I throw it. If something is True, it ought to feel as natural as a game of catch. There's a difference between having a learner's permit, where I know all the laws of traffic, and being an experienced driver. Even if I've forgotten some of the rules, we both know which one is safer. That's the difference between knowledge and understanding.

JENNY:

The formula seems to be everywhere. What if we changed it? What if we started out with the idea that we are right? We have everything inside of us already. If we just take a moment to be still and quiet we'll find the answers that we're looking for. Maybe it's time to start with trust instead of doubt.

DIETER:

Teachers are good, but the best ones are those who inspire you rather than try to give you something you don't have. What if instead of looking to a distant guru, we learned how to listen to our hearts?

JENNY:

Nobody deserves to live in ignorance of how they feel. You come with a natural warning system. Why not believe in it and use it to help guide you to a better life? Honor those feelings.

DIETER:

If that's the case, then it frees us up to make a difference, right where we are. Many heroes ride off into the sunset or go out into the wilderness. The great ones are those who come back and help. Right here and now, this life, this experience, is beautiful and worth fixing.

JENNY:

You are enough. The world is good. You have access to the answers. Your thoughts and feelings can guide you in healing ways. So you are good in potential and in expression.

THE NEW APPROACH:

- You are Right
- Listen to your Heart
- Trust your Feelings
- World Affirmation
- Self Worth

DIETER:

I love this inverted formula. It breaks free of the old cycle and makes your participation in any system, or relationship, or vocation, or whatever else, evolutionary and worthwhile.

JENNY:

I'm reminded of when Jesus told the disciples to cast their nets on the other side of the boat. He didn't start by telling them they were wrong, or that they didn't have what it took. One of the important things here is that Jesus doesn't tell the disciples they're bad for wanting to fish. Instead, He tells them how to do it better. The inference here is this approach makes you a better fisherman. The goal isn't escape or denial. There is too much work to do for that kind of foolishness. These ideas make you good at life. And *that* is what we want.

DIETER:

There's nothing to lose. What might seem like a loss is just external authority falling away. Somebody else's idea of success and failure isn't nearly as important as your inner guidance. Let's set aside the childish idea that there is a way to lose. After that, you can only succeed.

QUESTION HELPS

1. What rules do you live by? Which ones are explicit, and which are unspoken?
2. Is it okay to ask questions and demand answers that make sense to your head and heart? What will it take to get to a place of comfort with examination?
3. Where do your rules come from? Do some archaeology here. When they come from the outside, instead of from the inside, how does that feel?
4. Everybody has rules. Does being aware of yours help or hurt your ability to communicate and learn from other people?
5. Your prayer is your intention; your fundamental paradigm. What happens if you start with the idea that you are right; that you have access to all the answers, love, and victory you need?

CHAPTER TWO: LOVE

Every problem, big or small, has its root in a mindset of abstraction, separation, and duality. The solution is to cultivate a consciousness of love. That awareness will transcend thought and move into feeling, and from there will inspire the actions that make a loving, empowering life for all concerned.

SEE:

Find ways to see universal unity working in and through yourself, your work, your relationships, and your world. Look for the connection between subject, object, and ultimate concern.

SPEAK:

Act in ways that will break down boundaries and eliminate layers of abstraction. Show the world what love looks like.

SURRENDER:

Love is not about ego or personal will. Stop thinking about love and start letting love tell you what it has in store.

DIETER:

Last time around we talked about rewriting the old formulas. First of all, growth starts with consciousness; when you become aware that you are living by a lousy script, you can start to change it. The change starts to kick in when you know that you already have what it takes to grow. Many people don't have those two pieces of information. We know about the first part now. The second part is easy to prove. You have what it takes to grow because you want to grow. Evolution, discovery, adventure, and growth call to everyone. The fact that somewhere, maybe somewhere deep, there is a yearning to be better, is evidence of potential. From there, you can trust your heart. Your current thoughts and feelings can tell you what you need to move forward. There are clues in your situation right here and now. You may not have what you need to finish, but you have what it takes to start.

The secret, in and through everything else, is to look past the appearances and see the Truth. Facts change, but Truth is eternal. If you can get to the idea behind the thing, you have the key to moving forward past current circumstances, even when they feel hurtful.

JENNY:

I know that when I'm right in the middle of having a tough time it feels hard to look past appearances. Sometimes I just want to be angry for a minute before I start to think about how to make the situation better. You're right. The key to getting out of that place of hurt is to remember it's not the thing, it's the idea. When we experience pain in our lives it's usually easy to point out where we *think* the problem is coming from. It could be another person, work, sickness, financial trouble, etc. But there's something these all have in common. They are symptoms. Fixing the individual manifestations of that larger thing won't offer a permanent solution. Digging deeper and figuring out the cause is where the real healing begins.   The real problem we are facing is fear.

DIETER:

Yes!   Fear is the real feeling behind every other bad feeling, every negative experience.   When we are afraid, we give our power away.   Fear sets us apart, when a connection is where the power is.   When somebody has anger, frustration, hate, they are experiencing flavors of fear.   That's the core negative feeling.

We can go even deeper, though.   Every feeling starts with an idea.   The idea behind the feeling of fear is separation.   Being set apart, having a sense of dualism, is the cause.   If I feel separate from my good, I now have made room to be afraid.   That's where the whole thing starts.   If I believe that there is enough to go around, that I am enough, I change things.   If I know that good itself is omnipresent, what is there to be afraid of?

The average person tolerates many layers of abstraction just to get through the day. We work not because it's a labor of love, but because we'll get paid. We want that money not because there's anything inherently good about it. It's just paper. Even the things we buy with the money aren't what we want; it's what those things represent to us. This goes pretty deep. Think about how far the average person is from a direct experience of good, or Truth, or beauty. The feeling of alienation is where the problem starts.

Unfortunately, in our culture people wear their abstractions as merit badges. Sometimes we think of a successful person as one who has a lot of extracurricular activities. A winner is somebody who is able to put up with stress. We learn that a bulging to-do list is the mark of a good life.

JENNY:

Think about how that makes you feel. Maybe we need to work on a healthier definition of the word "prosperity." What is it that you want? Is it money? Is it attention? Or is it peace and harmony? Maybe real prosperity looks more like freedom. Maybe it is the power to have authentic experiences. When you chew on that for a while, you'll see that prosperity is inversely proportional to the layers of abstraction you allow.

Everybody wants to find oneness, to connect. Success comes from honoring this deep-seated drive. And failure comes from not acknowledging it. There's an interesting equation here. If you don't find the emotional connection you crave, you will create an equal amount of emotional distance. The numbers don't change.

DIETER:

Everybody knows somebody who is an example of that crazy math. I've lived out the equation myself. I can think back to some pretty bleak times in my life. I now see that I was putting up with situations and pursuits without any passion. The lost excitement has to go someplace. It turns into anger and separation. That distance and duality make life feel worse, so there's more room for bad ideas and bad choices. The cycle continues. Separation is at the core of every other bad thing. If we can fix that, everything else gets fixed, too.

JENNY:

There are a lot of different ways to get to a solution. Different people have different approaches and ideas. We look for a better job. We exercise. We get a bigger house or a faster car. We get better at self care. That is wonderful, but it is not a cure. If the underlying feeling doesn't change, the problem will just manifest in different ways. The goal of therapy, spirituality, or healing is not to get tougher so that you can deal with a terrible life. If we're doing it right, we find tools to make life better. The problem starts with an idea. We've talked about that. The answer has to do with getting back to an idea, too. We know where bad feelings start. Where do your good feelings come from? Everything you want, that makes you feel better, that inspires you, has a big idea in common. The idea is love.

DIETER:

There it is. You are right, of course. When love is authentic, it is the solution. But for love to be the answer to anything, for it to be the fulfillment of the law and the thing that makes the world go 'round, we need to know what it is not. Contrary to popular belief, love has nothing to do with being weak. Being loving is not the same as being a doormat. Sometimes folks misinterpret the "turn the other cheek" idea and equate love with an ability to endure abuse.

JENNY:

It's also not just the mushy stuff that we see in movies or read in novels. We see this cultural definition of love when people come to us for relationship advice. So often, the problem really is that people date an actual human being, when they had a fairytale in mind. Those stories paint a superficial picture, and end before anything real happens. They never show you what happens after "true love's kiss" ends and real life begins. They don't prepare us for depth, and they teach us that we must adore every aspect of the other person. Even when they are acting like jerks.

DIETER:

Love has been shorthand for codependency for a long time. Some folks think that if you love somebody enough, you will put up with all kinds of dysfunction. That's not love, it's a deception. If, through my behavior, I'm validating your bad decisions and hurtful conduct, I'm letting you believe a lie. I'm letting you think it's okay to be less than who you really are. That's not what friends do.

It makes me think of the word "namaste." Don't get me wrong here; that's a lovely word and people who use it do so with good intentions. It means something like "the best in me sees the best in you," and I love that. That *best* part can get left out of the mix. For some people the namaste attitude means a wholesale validation of the outer situation. No effort to behold transcendent Truth there. It's more like "the mundane in me puts up with the mundane in you," which lets us hold still instead of encouraging us to grow.

JENNY:

It's nice to know what love isn't, but to understand something you must define it. So what is love?

DIETER:

Love is a power that moves. When you feel it, you can't hold still, and it causes you to want to do and be more. Love breaks boundaries. When you have an idea about love, it transcends thought and becomes feeling. The feeling of love overflows into action. None of us can help it. That's only the beginning. Once love gets out into the world, it starts knocking down walls.

When we do wedding ceremonies, we usually read from 1 Corinthians 13. There's a lot in there, and it's all beautiful. Most people miss the real point of the reading, though. The key is that "love rejoices in the Truth." Of course love shouldn't be judgemental or superficial. Of course love and acceptance should go hand in hand. Love is the best part of us. Seeing with the eyes of love means that we insist on the best from ourselves and try to inspire it in others.

In other words, I love you so much I'm not going to put up with less than the Truth from you. That's what love rejoices in. I love and accept you, but I don't need your ego, your fear, your dysfunction. Those things aren't who you really are; putting up with them is not love. It's a lie. Like we said, the problem, behind any individual manifestation, is abstraction. Love tears down those walls. Love does not allow, it *demands*.

JENNY:

Love is at the core of our human operating system. You could say that we are connection engines. We've already talked about our inherent desire to connect. We want to find common ground with one another. It is the language we speak.

It's not just that we want to bond. Those connections help form our identities. You don't know a person, place, or thing by itself. You define it, at least in part, by understanding its relationship to the rest of the world. We know ourselves in the context of the greater whole. There's a theory out there that you are the average of the five people that you hang around with the most.

Love is proof that we are inherently good. You could take a person who has had the worst background imaginable. Someone who has never experienced love in their lives. Imagine that they have been through the worst version of every life story ever written. Pretend that this person has never had any experience of love. Even *that* person can tell you what love is, if they are still enough, quiet enough, and honest enough. The definition and understanding comes from something we all have inside us. Even if we've never experienced it on the outside.

DIETER:

Whenever people talk about love they are talking about a connection. When you love something, you are experiencing a kind of oneness with it. People say "I love that shirt, it's really you!" Part of dating has to do with figuring out how much the two people have in common. It's a great start.

Here again, though, we want to drill down past the superficial and into the heart of things. A good relationship isn't based around whether you both agree that Patrick Stewart was a better captain of the Enterprise. Something more profound has to be there for things to evolve and survive. Real love, love taken all the way, involves another element. It's not just that you and I are one, but that you and I are participating in something bigger than either of us. It doesn't matter what name you give that bigger something. It can be Spirit, or God, or Truth, or Beauty. Real love is a radical connection between subject, object, and ultimate concern. That's what it is all about.

If you want a healthy relationship, try to work past the drudgery of everyday life. You are more than the things that you have to do, so your ultimate concern has to be bigger still. Find a connection with a higher love. If you want to be successful at work, try to labor with a sense of mission. Anything you do is better with love as the guide. Whatever you're doing, give it the laser beam intensity of your full self. Give it love. If you've tried to apply love and things aren't changing, the message might be that it's time to move on. Either way, starting with love is the way forward. Abstraction and distance keep us in stasis. Passionate honesty and authenticity dispel the abstraction. They tell us what we need to grow in a situation or get out of it.

JENNY:

The way to grow is to celebrate love. That seems like a tall order, but the good news is that you can start small. Start thinking about love in any way that you can. It doesn't matter if it's a silly thing, like thinking about the way you feel when you see puppies. Just start where you are. Over time, you'll give yourself permission to see love happening on a more profound level. Become the kind of person who goes around looking for examples of love. Sooner or later you'll get to the point where things change.

Incorporate love into your vocabulary. It's easy to focus on upsetting or frustrating elements in life, but that attention won't make them go away. You can choose to place your focus elsewhere, though. If love becomes the thing that catches your attention, something happens. Your focus on love will break down a boundary for you. Instead of standing on the outside, looking at examples of love, you'll show the world what love looks like. You won't be a person thinking *about* love in an abstract way, but rather you'll be *thinking* love. It's a "what would love do?" situation.

Life is a spiral, where a bad decision leads to a bad experience which leads to another bad decision. Choosing love is all it takes to reverse direction. Love begets love. A loving decision will create a positive experience, which makes it even easier to show love. The gravitational power of love will change things. It really does make the world go around. They call it falling in love, because it's like gravity. We have a choice about the direction. We just have to let it be in charge.

DIETER:

All that love cares about, all that it sees, is love itself. Here's the mantra: *Love just loves.* Sometimes we cry or feel frustrated. Sometimes we get angry.

All those feelings are valid. But they're not love. They're something else. It might be ego or the desire to control. It's often the realization that things need to unfold differently than our expectations.

Love just loves. If we give ourselves over to that primal force, we see that it is unstoppable. We become unstoppable, too. The power doesn't have to come from us anymore. It can flow through us. Remove your pretension and be honest. Release your expectations and listen. The answer is already here.

QUESTION HELPS

1. Look past material details. What do all of your negative experiences have in common? What is the problem?
2. What, then, is the solution? What do all of your positive experiences and feelings have in common?
3. What are some ways in which you can cultivate an appreciation for the various occurrences and examples of love, big and small, in everyday life?
4. Take an inventory of the kinds of abstractions you encounter at home and at work. Can you find some small ways to break through the abstractions and forge connections to Truth, beauty, or happiness?
5. How can you show the world what love looks like?

CHAPTER THREE: SELF

You are more than your possessions, accomplishments, or outer conditions. Happiness and fulfillment come from embracing the permanent transcendent Truth manifesting through temporal outer experience.

SEE:

Remember that your current material situation is only a manifestation of a deeper, more profound, infinite Truth.

SPEAK:

Find ways to let your real self show through each thought, word, and action.

SURRENDER:

Celebrate the changes you experience; they are just making room for a bigger experience of life.

DIETER:

A big part of the growth process has to do with a sense of self. You can learn a lot if you give some thought to where your identity comes from. What do you want to show the world? What do you currently claim? What relationships and other factors contribute to your definition of who you are? In other words, *where do you get your "you" from?* There are many competing and contributing sources of identity. Not all of them are particularly healthy. A person might derive their identity from their job, but when they retire or get laid off there's a problem. You can define yourself by what you have, what you do, or who you're with, but there are issues there.

The "who am I?" question is one we are born trying to answer. I think that we start out asking it, but, even more, life is asking us. In one way or the other, that's what every moment of existence is about. Can you figure out who you are and share it with the world? That's what we are all here to do. Even if we are not aware of that calling, the hunger is there.   It's even something that is marketed to. Commercials sell you a new and improved version of yourself more than they are selling a product. Getting you to identify with, and thereby become dependent on, a new product is part of the game. We also see this in work, in relationships, and even in some religions.

The common answers to the question have to do with labels. Labels are by definition external. Labels tend to work from outside in, which hardly ever feels right.   More than that, labels are always stationary, versus dynamic or evolutionary. Most people choose or get a sense of identity that enables them to hold still. What they want is one that encourages them to move forward.

JENNY:

It's so easy to feel that we are what we own. As they say, though, your possessions can end up owning you. That never lasts. For me, the lesson was pretty severe.

When I was around ten years old, I went through a profound experience. My mom was leaving an abusive marriage. I remember we had to leave the house in the middle of the night and only take what would fit in a small suitcase. I remember grabbing my pillow. I can't tell you why that was important to me now but then it seemed like the thing to bring. We got to safety and started a new life in Florida. When my stepfather found out we were gone he sold everything he could of what we left behind. What he couldn't sell, he burned. I lost the dolls and clothes my grandma made for me. I lost my girl scout badges that I had worked so hard to get. I lost several things that were important to a ten year old.

After we got away, I remember snuggling with my grandma and thinking that maybe I didn't have the things she made, but I had her. I may not have had my badges but I was always going to be a girl scout. My memories and achievements did not go away. The Truth about me only became more clear.

It is a moment fixed in time, but I am no longer in that place. Life has a way of moving you forward in grace if you allow it. Some people define themselves by what they have, but that's absurd. You were *you* before you got that house, car, or diamond ring. It could go away, and you would remain. I think many people have stories like mine. The choice we all have is to feel bad about it, or to move past the grief and say "it's gone, but here I am." That's a powerful lesson. It may just be that the universe needed a more honest version of us. We are not defined by what we own. If it can go away, it's not the Truth.

DIETER:

One way or the other, that lesson comes. We learn, the easy way or the hard way, that things can't tell us who we are. This is important. In pop spirituality, there is so much attention paid to attraction and manifestation. I think that some folks focus so much on that end of things that they forget that it is only one end. They think that material things are the end-all and be-all of spiritual work. I love the feeling that comes from having dreams and prayers realized in manifestation. I never want to forget how things work, though. I don't want to start attributing power to the things that are created. That's golden calf spirituality.

There's nothing wrong with having things. We can do a great deal of good in the world with them. The creative act is powerful, but once we create a thing, there's no more power in it. It's just stuff; it's like a dead battery. Getting wrapped up in materiality is like fixating on the rabbit after he's been pulled out of the hat. Better to be the kind of person who appreciates what happened, but is ready to hear "and now for my next trick."

JENNY:

So it's not the stuff we have, and it's not even what we did to get the stuff. We are not defined by our actions or accomplishments. On one level it feels good to have goals in mind, and it's great to reach those finish lines. But if that becomes who I am, rather than just what I do, there's no end to the striving. It's exhausting, because nothing is ever good enough. Achievements are wonderful, but letting them tell us who we are is tricky. Attainments are in the past, but the attitude that craves them is always looking to the future. If that's the paradigm, right here and now, we don't have whatever brass ring we're currently reaching for. It's hard to feel anything but anxious when you're in limbo.

If all you are is what you do, what happens when you're not doing anything? Again we go back to the idea that anything external isn't going to fill that space inside your heart. Work and mission are important, but they are just small parts of how we should be defining ourselves.

DIETER:

Actions are good; the goal here is not stagnation. None of this means much if we don't do something about it. That's the end of the process, however, and in some ways the least important part. The things we do are significant, but only as indicators of something deeper.

Put another way, of course we want to do something about what we feel and know. But those actions should be the natural result of ideas that are too big to be contained, like love. In the same way, the identity that the world sees should be the natural manifestation of an inner Truth. It should not be an outer mask that we hope will hide or change something deeper.

Some people are in a hurry to put on a series of external labels. Those people are looking for a destination so that they can hold still. People are sold the idea that they ought to be looking for a finish line. If you're living your life so that you can *stop* living, you're making bad choices along the way. Everything you are doing now is practice for what you will be doing later. If you practice action, you won't get good at stillness. If you practice misery, you won't become an expert at happiness.   External labels are destinations, and what you want is the journey.

When you think about it, you can chart every hero story on a map; Lord of the Rings, Exodus, and so on. Heros move. Motion is what we want, and it's what we are.   We are born to grow and evolve. Somebody sold us the idea that we should want to hold still, but that's a cheapshot.   If we shoot for stagnation, we are easy to control. It can't last long, however, because it's not the Truth.   That's why we always rebel against that kind of oppression.

JENNY:

Remember when I was pregnant with our kids? Each time, towards the end it was miserable.   The baby gets big and there is just no more room. It got to the point where even though I knew that labor would be difficult and painful I looked forward to it. It works that way in life too. Whether or not you're physically pregnant, a new life is always calling. No one can tolerate staying in an uncomfortable situation forever. We can only put up with stasis for so long. Life will force us to move.

There is a simple misunderstanding at the root of this stagnation problem. The transcendent Truth about you, the divine spark, your spiritual nature, is unchanging. You are permanent on the inside and in the ultimate. In the outer, in manifestation, you are in process. Everything about your outer condition is in a constant state of flux, even on a microscopic level. Material things change, as everyone knows. Even though everybody knows that, a lot of people spend a lot of time looking for permanence in the wrong place.

DIETER:

Even if it's vague, we all have a notion that we have an eternal, permanent nature. Everybody is hungry for a deeper experience of it. The problem happens when we look for permanence in superficial things. We are bound to be disappointed, unless and until we learn how to see with different eyes. The trick to being open to outer process is in grasping inner permanence.   If you feel disappointed, it probably means that you're looking for stability where it cannot exist.   Your outer condition is process.   Embrace it, instead of trying to make it something that it is not. We are warned not to build on a foundation of shifting sand. If we can be okay with the changing nature of manifestation, we can get a better grip on the permanent, transcendent Truth behind it.

God does not have trouble with this.   The universe takes care of its own. If there's resistance in my life, where is it? Is God doing it? Is the universe having a hard time making good happen? Of course not. Here's the hard lesson: *Every friction you feel is you trying to hold still when life is trying to pull you ahead.* But that's a choice.

The friction is a beautiful thing. It's wonderful to feel that resistance, because we can use it to be reminded what is important. It's amazing to feel loss, because we are forced to deal with real permanence and find it in a healthier place. Every moment really is a gift.

JENNY:

The labels I agree with, whether I choose them or not, form my identity, the sign I carry. The goal is to work on a sense of identity that mirrors a transcendent Truth. I want to identify with something bigger and more beautiful than my current situation. But identity is only half of the equation. The real test is living with authenticity.

This is about learning who you really are. It's about an identity that comes from the inside and shines out. Who you are is not glued on from the outside. You grasp your real self through moments of authenticity. In other words, when you do or experience things that are inherently worthwhile, they reveal what's True. We want to feel a sense of self that is not mediated by externals. Try and do things that are *good*, independent of what other people say or what the results might be. These moments give us clues about who or what we might become.

Healing and growth can happen if we just try to connect with those moments of authenticity. Find ways to seek them out, big and small. Get in touch with anything that takes you out of time. It can be art, music, time with family, meditation, anything. Get in the habit of it, and you'll start to get better at it. You'll start expressing who you are, instead of what you have or what you do.

It feels easy to spend your life, and I do mean *spend* it, hiding from those moments. It feels easy to go through the motions and not connect with emotions. But it's the hardest thing there is. Hiding is difficult, because it keeps our good hidden. There is one thing, at least one thing, that you can do or think about that feels real, beyond the shifting sands of opinion or changing circumstances. That is where you'll find your gift -- the thing you alone are here to do. If you can use the example of your life to show the world where to find something real, you will prosper.

DIETER:

There's that wonderful passage in Scripture. Jesus asks the disciples what labels people are putting on Him. He asks "who do they say that I am?" He gets back some definitions based on external data or secondhand expectations. Then He asks the disciples "who do *you* say that I am?" Peter, the disciple who represents Faith, says "I say that you are the Christ, the Son of the living God." Jesus pats Peter on the back, pointing out that "flesh and blood has not revealed this answer" to him, which is why it's the right one.

There's a lot going on there. The essence of it is that it takes faith, the power that sees past appearances and into potentiality, the power that sees through fact and into Truth, to see that there is a living divine nature behind, above, and beyond any external labels.

In that OTHER scripture that I hold near and dear to my heart, Star Wars, there's that part where Luke turns off his targeting computer. He does it because the voice of his teacher Obi Wan, itself beyond material perception, tells him "trust your feelings." They are saying the same thing in different ways.

Remember that Jesus says of Peter "upon this rock I will build my church." I take that to mean that faith, the power to see deeper, is where this whole thing has to start. Our definition of self has to begin within.

JENNY:

Your heart is a wonderful barometer. Your feelings are yours and they are real. Even if they are negative, your feelings are valid. Not only the good happy emotions help you grow. Feelings are not mediated by external elements; you feel how you feel. Your perceptions may be filtered in all kinds of ways, but how you feel is not.

Your feelings may not be the facts about what's happening outside of you. They are a perfect representation of where you're at on the inside, though. Your feelings can help get to the Truth by telling you something about how you process your experience. Your feelings can tell you about your baggage and your bias.

DIETER:

It's not just what's happening, but rather how you *feel* about what's happening. Your feelings can tell you a little bit more about where you're at, which in turn can help you get where you want to go. They can help you figure out where the walls are between your transcendent True identity and its current temporal manifestation. When you feel angry or afraid, you are experiencing the disconnect between your facts and the Truth. Once you know that, you can grow.

If you can be okay with being in outer process because of your inner Truth, you're on the right track.

QUESTION HELPS

1. Make a list of the labels you carry, and the places that those labels come from. Where do you get your "you" from?
2. When you have experienced the feeling of loss, what did you lose, given that you are still here?
3. What's the difference between having goals and being defined by your achievements?
4. When you feel friction in your life, where does it come from?
5. What can your feelings tell you about who you really are?

CHAPTER FOUR: RELATIONSHIPS

There are no accidents. The people
in your life are with you to learn
from you and also to teach you. If
you can seize the educational
opportunity, you will be a good
friend and partner.

SEE:

Know that there is one Truth, but give thanks that we are each on our own unique path of expression.

SPEAK:

Seize the educational opportunities present in each relationship, and work to behold and inspire transcendence and love.

SURRENDER:

Recognize that you are a mirror to the people in your life, and they are the same for you. Practice the Golden Rule, and trust the unfolding process.

JENNY:

We know a little bit about identity and authenticity now. The real test is application; how can we take what we've learned and apply it to relationships? What does it take to be a friend? I think there are many possible answers. The way a person deals with that question tells us quite a bit about who they are and where they're at. What somebody is looking for and what they're willing to contribute reveals a lot. The contribution part is vital, even though it is often overlooked. We can define friendship as what a person is able to share, and how they encourage others to do the same. Inspiration is the key to a healthy friendship.

Right here and now you and I are in transition, in the outer. We know that. I'm a good friend and partner if I, in my current process, can reflect or remind you about eternal Truth. As we've said, the trick is to look past the temporal process and into timeless transcendence. If we can see that about ourselves, we can behold it in others, too. That's the basis of something healthy and beautiful.

DIETER:

Sharing is what it's all about. The quality of any relationship is in inverse proportion to how much the participants are holding back. One phrase that drives me crazy is "I love you, but." When I hear any variation of that, what I hear is fear. To me, it sounds like something is kept in reserve for self-protection. It sounds like somebody's keeping score. When you love someone, you don't have to completely buy into everything about them. You can love somebody but not agree with the way they live a part of their lives. That part doesn't have to come up for you every time you think of them. Nobody else is keeping track.

As an individual, I should be working on everything I say, do, and think. I'm in process in those areas. Hopefully I can get to the point where I'm willing to stand behind everything I'm putting out there. That's for my growth. That's my path.

There is no point where I should hold others to my standard, though.

Just love. Love to the point where you don't need the other person to be a clone of yourself. Your differences don't have to come out, and they don't have to define either of you. Real love has to do with looking past the details and into the oneness. No single wrong move or undesirable characteristic should define a person. Movie villains are written that way because the story has to be told in ninety minutes and we need clear-cut good and bad guys. This is not the movies.

Besides, the differences are there to show us that love is more than details. They are there to teach us to look past facts and into the Truth. Be grateful for the educational opportunity.

JENNY:

That's an important point. What's the Mother Teresa saying? "Some people come into your life as blessings. Some come into your life as lessons." I think that we pick our relationships based on how ready we are to move through what they are trying to teach us. We pick our relationships on the level of soul choice and readiness. There are no accidents. Without exception, each person in your life is there for two reasons: They are there to learn from you, and they are there to teach you. People flow into and out of your life based on how ready you are to receive the message the universe is trying to convey through your interaction with them.

It's important to acknowledge that we play a part in manifesting people in our lives. You get the people you're ready for, but that readiness can mean different things. Some teachers show what to do, and some demonstrate what not to do. We either come to a mutual understanding and walk life's path together or we move on from each other. The tricky part is figuring out when to stay and when to go.

How someone makes you feel can guide whether you should continue a relationship. Of course I'm not talking about an occasional argument or disagreement. That's going to happen. I'm talking about the general trend of how you feel when you're around that person. Sometimes we find people who inspire and challenge us with courage and Truth. Sometimes we find people who force us to demand better treatment.

With all due respect to Mother Teresa, I think everybody is both. They're a blessing, or they're a lesson, but the lesson is a blessing, too. And what's a blessing, if it isn't also a lesson?

DIETER:

Part of the geographical cure theory has to do with the idea that the same personalities will come up over and over again. You might leave that spouse or quit the job. Until you learn and teach, you'll get in the same relationships with different people. I know that every person on the planet has direct experience with this. The way out has to do with seizing the educational opportunity and doing your best. If you leave before that, you'll just have to do it over, perhaps with a different person, but it's still the same cycle. It won't change until *you* do, and you might as well start with what you've got.

Pulling the ripcord is not a good first reaction. We have to be able to say we have given love. We have to be able to say that we've done our best to model Truth. If we can, the decision to grow together or apart usually gets made by itself. We just have to give with an open heart. It's about the Golden Rule, which also implies being proactive.

JENNY:

It means giving without attachment to the outcome or the reaction. I've learned this lesson a few times in my life. I've had plenty of opportunities to deal with the same type of difficult personality over and over again. In every case, I'd just be going along, living my life, and here they would come. Sometimes it seemed like they couldn't stand the sight of me, let alone have any kind of relationship. Sometimes I was glad to see them come into my life, and sometimes I was overjoyed to see them go. I went through times where I questioned what I might have done to make them so angry. The process always involved a blame phase for me. That relationship cycle didn't change until I realized that it wasn't about me at all. I decided to just do my best and stop tying myself into knots trying to read other people's minds.

I think that we can act as a mirror for others. Their issues are about them, just as mine are about me. Whether we want the job or not, sometimes others choose us to be their teachers. Maybe we represent a part of their lives they are healing. It's not helpful or friendly to start hiding that part in response to their difficulty. Instead, the trick is to keep trying to show love. At the same time, we have to remember that real love is not conditioned by a response.

You are a mirror. So is the other person. It's important to remember that we can help each other grow by what we reflect. Let's get as good at that as

we can.   Take the opportunity to grow.   Clean the
mirror.

DIETER:

I love the idea of taking responsibility.   When
there's static in a relationship, sometimes the
problem has to do with putting somebody else in
charge of your happiness.   That's a losing
proposition.   By the same token, you can't make
yourself responsible for somebody else's happiness,
either.   That misplacement of power, that confusion
of source, constructs a false idol.   There's a
commandment about that.   Life, friendship, and
everything else has to do with the spirit of that law.
It's about seeing something higher.   Neither of us is
the source of happiness.   We take part in it together.
It's the music we dance to.

JENNY:

You can't expect people to *be* you or to read your
mind.   Trouble can start if you need someone to

know every single one of your thoughts, or vice-versa. So often this is where a problem starts. Would you want someone that was exactly like you? A clone? I think that's a little creepy. Would you want to be in a relationship with yourself? What you're looking for is compatibility, not duplication. That's vastly different.

DIETER:

We can look for carbon copies of each other, but there's no room for learning there. We can get hung up on the differences, but at best we can only learn what *not* to do. Or we can try and communicate what's in our hearts. The teaching is to "let your yes be yes, and your no be no." Just as we've said before, love rejoices with the Truth. Being a friend and partner means acting in integrity. In love, but in Truth. I want to know where I stand with you, and you deserve the same from me.

JENNY:

We have to tell our truth, and we have to tell it quickly. Holding back on communication can end up being a lie. Remember that Truth is not about superficial things, it's about what's ultimate and real. That kind of Truth cannot hurt. It's keeping it quiet that can do damage.

It can seem like a hard thing to do at first. Once you start to make this a habit you'll see the benefits far outweigh the risks. Of course it would be ideal if you could deliver your truth in a peaceful way. Because we're all human, this is not always possible. Do the best you can but always be genuine and don't let that moment pass.

DIETER:

Practice active and passive honesty. Don't participate in a falsehood. "No" is a magic word. It liberates and empowers. Creativity comes from constraints, for one thing. More than that, "no" is a loving word. Think of how many talent-based reality shows where the "fun" is pretty mean-spirited. It has to do with laughing at how bad some of the contestants are. I can't watch that kind of thing; it makes me sad. I want to say "didn't somebody love you enough to tell you not to do this?" There are so many stories of celebrities who have surrounded themselves with people who tell them that everything they do is genius. It's the beginning of so much craziness. It's also why the Star Wars prequels are dreadful.

JENNY:

"No" is powerful, even if it seems negative. It reminds me of what I'd say to a misbehaving child. When you discipline a kid, they might say "you don't like me." A good parent would say something like "I love you, but I'm not crazy about your behavior. Let's have what you do be a better match to who you are." One way or the other, this is about getting past the superficial parts of you. We've said that you are not your actions or your possessions; we want to share our True identities.

There's a great picture of the galaxy in all its hugeness. There's an arrow pointing to the Earth, which is tiny in this perspective. The idea is that my material self and issues are insignificant. On a physical level, none of this matters. To get to what matters, we have to see things in a different way. To make a real connection with somebody, look for what you have in common in an ultimate sense, rather than what is superficial.

DIETER:

The key to life in general and relationships in particular is to find something bigger than you. Something bigger than both of you. I don't take out the garbage or do the dishes for you. I do it for our marriage, which is bigger than the two of us. It means a sense of mission, and it keeps either of us from being the source of good or the judge of worth. Love should not come from us, but through us. If we can celebrate together and aim higher together, we give ourselves freedom to grow together.

JENNY:

Keeping a high watch is key. Seeing the Truth past the facts lets us stay open. We connect differently to different people. We might share a material connection, like being from the same family or working in the same place. We may have a similar background or like the same kinds of food. That's fine, but it's not especially deep, so it's not especially durable. A deeper connection is on the moral or intellectual level. We approach the world the same way; maybe we vote the same way or read the same books. It's a bit deeper, and at least we have something more interesting to talk about. But it's still a dualistic situation; it's you and me. The magic happens when the duality goes away. We experience oneness when we start to participate in that something bigger. It's a spiritual connection.

DIETER:

Those types of connections have to happen in the right sequence in order for them to be authentic. You have to have that spiritual connection and let it inspire and flow through the other two.

JENNY:

Spiritual connection is *not* the same as having the same faith claim. It just means that you have the same "bigger thing" in mind, even if you express it differently.

DIETER:

It's vital to ask what your journey is, and just as important to ask who will walk it with you. It's even more important to make sure you tackle those issues in the correct order. If you look for partners and validation first, you won't be able to figure out your mission. That can only lead to frustration. You won't be able to see that "bigger thing" the way that you need to.

JENNY:

Starting with a sense of calling, with a higher goal, frees you up to be a better friend and partner. You'll inevitably draw others to yourself who are on that level. If you're the kind of person who is looking for Truth, it's easier to find that in others, too. Along the way, that higher purpose will be easier for other people to see.

DIETER:

There are no accidents in the universe. You are a deliberate creation, and you are unique and essential. You are here to tell your story.

JENNY:

And you are here to listen. How do you feel when you hear somebody else's story? This is not about tolerating different points of view. This is about *celebrating*. Can you celebrate somebody else's story, in the knowing that you're looking for the deep

Truth behind the appearances? This is important, because you get more of what you focus on. If you fixate on the problems and differences, you aren't blazing a trail to harmony. If you can celebrate, not with words, but with passion and intention, everybody gets a chance to grow. What people are doing isn't about you, anyhow. It's an expression of what they are working on. If you get hung up on the problems, you're not helping their inner Truth to come out. Can you find a way to behold it, perhaps through teaching by example?

DIETER:

What are you about? Part of this is has to do with finding yourself so that you have something to share beyond outer expectations. What makes you tick? Share that, and applaud it in others, and you're on the way to a real partnership.

QUESTION HELPS

1. What does it take to be a friend?
2. Think about the most profound relationships you've had. Is there a discernable pattern? What can you learn and teach?
3. What are some situations where your "no" is the best way to be authentic?
4. What is your journey? Do you have friendships that support that path?
5. Is there a "bigger thing" or transcendent concept manifested through your closest relationships? How can you discern and express it?

CHAPTER FIVE: FAMILY

Your tribe is determined by vision
and intention. Together, you are
what you serve. Finding a bigger
idea is the path to unity, healing, and
growth.

SEE:

Beyond and though material circumstances, family is united and defined by service.   Look for the Truth within that common ground.

SPEAK:

Find ways to uplift and expand your idea of service, and work to demonstrate that vision in action.

SURRENDER:

Leave room to learn from the examples of others as they follow their paths, and celebrate the diversity of understanding and expression.

JENNY:

We know that there are no accidents. There just isn't room for them in the universe. That's easy to get a grip on when we talk about our friendships. On one level or another we consciously choose the people we are friends with. We've talked about the idea that we are in each other's lives for educational reasons. We are here to learn and to teach. If you can take the reins there, and consciously choose to be a student and a teacher, you'll enrich your relationships.

This is the next level. Choice doesn't *just* happen on a conscious level, as you know. That means that, know it or not, and like it or not, you've chosen the people in your family. This typically is not a choice we're aware of. Instead, it happens as a result of soul readiness. In fact, sometimes the people in our family are better teachers than our friends. They've been with us longer, for one thing. More than that, we didn't choose them on purpose, we chose them on a deeper level. That deeper level is what we're trying to unearth. Family is powerful.

DIETER:

The word itself can mean a lot of things. Broadly, "family" refers to a set of objects with shared characteristics. True, but not especially enlightening. The material or biological connection is valid. We've been thinking through this for long enough to know that our physicality is the least important part of us, though. "Family" can also refer to your household. Getting warmer, there, because that's not just a physical connection. There's something happening on an emotional level. But there's more to explore.

Surprisingly enough, another definition that is even more instructive is the notion of a *crime* family. That's another thing people think of when they hear the word, and there's actually some power there. I haven't been watching too many Coppola movies. The reason I like that last one is that it includes physical proximity and characteristics, and it also includes emotional connections. More than that, though, it denotes some kind of shared purpose. In the movies, it's a negative vision, but it's still evidence of something deeper.

Looking at something on a material level is fine, but anything manifest is just evidence of the past. Emotions are good, too, but they can only tell us where we are right now. Vision, on the other hand, is the future. We're really talking about faith, and that's where the power is.

JENNY:

I find it interesting that the word "family" comes from from the latin *famulus*, meaning "servant." We serve something in common, and that is what makes us a family. More than anything physical, it's that idea of service that defines the relationship. The problem is that we can serve all kinds of things. Sometimes it's something noble, like love or honor. Sometimes a family unites around a particular addiction or dysfunction. The quality of the service, and the purity of what's being served, determines the health of the family.

Contrary to appearances, a family isn't physical or biological, really. You can be in a family with people who don't share any of your DNA, with people who don't share the same house. Family doesn't come from there. It is instead defined by purpose and action. You can't fix your family by forcing it to adhere to new outer conditions. Instead, if you don't like what's going on in your family, figure out what it's serving. See if that can't be refocused or changed. If you can change the service, you can change the tone and everything else.

DIETER:

One thing you don't have a choice about is being *in* a family. Humans are social creatures; we require the presence of others to survive. This is the case physically, emotionally, and spiritually, too. Nobody is alone. In fact, every individual fits into a pretty big network of overlapping families. This has been part of our makeup since the dawn of humanity, and I think it's getting more and more evident. Even though technology keeps delivering toys that are purported to isolate us, they are only attractive because they make connections. We use social networks and new technologies to enhance our feelings of belonging.

JENNY:

Naturally, I'd like to see the connections happen about something more profound than what we often see. I'll take what comes. It's a start. Even when the bond is over something superficial, it proves the desire for oneness. Those connections can be on Facebook or what we see over and over again in the Bible, where lineage has so much importance. Once again, let's not fix the material situation. Let's fix what we are serving. Our connections are what define us.

DIETER:

There's this great part in Joshua, chapter 24 verse 15, where the prophet says "Choose for yourselves today whom you will serve." The idea is that the people listening could choose to serve the old gods, even though they were limited to physical and geographical boundaries and subject to ego and whim. Then he says "...as for me and my house, we will serve the Lord." This whole part of Scripture is about the transmutation from belief in a local and contextual deity to a concept of a transcendent, omnipresent God. In a way, this is what we're doing right now. We are trying to change what our tribe, our family, is focused on. We want to move the focus of service from something small and petty to something that will help us get out of our own way. That's how to start growing in love.

Some people wonder why their families are repeating the same dysfunctional cycles, over and over again. This is a valid question. My reply is that there are tribes out in the middle of nowhere still doing what their ancestors did thousands of years ago. They have the same gods they had at the beginning. They serve the same thing, so of course they think, feel, and act the same way. You can't change the action until you change the vision. Change the service, and you'll change how you see yourself.

JENNY:

What are you, after all? If you are defined by your physicality, and your family is defined by your biology, you have a pretty limited definition. What if you're adopted? What if your family doesn't fit into a traditional understanding? Does that change the validity? Family can cause us to ask some pretty beautiful questions and get past some pretty ugly ideas.

There's another side to this. There are times when you've tried, but you just can't find common ground with the people in your family. You can want something esoteric, or it can be something simple, like health or safety. If family is material or even emotional, you're stuck. Lots of people can see a problem in their families, but they think that they have to live with it. Maybe you have a biological or psychological connection with people who are acting in toxic ways. That doesn't mean that *you* are toxic, too, just because you're related. Let's think about that for a second. If something hurts, that's proof that you don't have anything in common with it. That hurt can get you to a place of action.

If you allow yourself to define things on more transcendent terms, you might give yourself enough breathing room to either fix things or move on to a healthier place. Even a dysfunctional family can help teach you to see life in a different way. You may need to leave to get that lesson, but until you learn it you're going to feel frozen.

DIETER:

That's the power of family, ideally. Instead of holding you back, it can help break you out of material definitions and behavioral cycles. When family focuses on healthy service, it can lift us up and empower us.

I'm so proud of the agreement we've made with our children. When they were old enough to understand, we told them they didn't have to worry about rent or jobs or even grades, as long as they stayed curious and kept working to better themselves. As a result, they've gotten amazing grades and entered college at early ages. They're successes at everything they do. Most importantly, they're happy. For them, education won't stop with a degree or a milestone. Their journey will only keep going. It's absolutely guaranteed to evolve in directions that you and I will not understand. Whether we can wrap our heads around it or not isn't important. We have to trust.

The idea is that what we owe each other is honesty and respect, but we're not obliged to fit into each other's expectations. Growth comes from a celebration of the paths that others take to the service we have in common.

JENNY:

Celebration and family are supposed to go hand in hand. When you think about family gatherings, you're usually thinking about an observance of some rite of passage. We get together for birthdays and graduations, for weddings and funerals. Your family, biological or otherwise, is there with you as you go through the important transitions of life. Those observances show that we are still tribal people at our core. Typically, a tribal rite of passage is about a sacrifice of the personal in acknowledgement of the greater good. Sometimes that's what we see in modern family celebrations, too. When we do it right, it doesn't matter if cousin so-and-so is graduating from school in order to pursue a career we don't understand. What's important is that she's moving on and growing, so she's able to serve her higher purpose in a better way.

Sometimes people miss the point, and the celebration can be an affirmation that the younger generation is going to conform to old expectations. If everyone in your family is a doctor and you want to be a car mechanic it can be a challenge to get family members to see things differently. But that's precisely what needs to be done, for your sake as well as for theirs. You can be there to show your tribe that new and bigger ideas are possible. The answer is to recognize and celebrate similarities but also to leave room for the differences.

DIETER:

This whole journey is about embracing our outer situations, but at the same time seeing them as secondary. Where you are, in the outer, is just a manifestation of what you carry in your mind and heart. This is there in all areas of life, of course, but family is a great place to see it in action. If you limit yourself by externals, like traditions, genetics, and past experience, you will grow resentful. It hurts, because it's not the Truth. The frustration you feel is the friction of Truth trying to come out of a resistant mentality, a mindset stuck in old facts. You can let that go if you just decide that you're more than your circumstances. Life is calling for a revolutionary definition. We need a new sense of what we are about and what we really inherit.

JENNY:

Who are you, anyway? We can find new life and purpose when we just remember that our nature is transcendent, not physical. Sure, you might have your father's nose. With enough money and the right plastic surgeon, you can change that. It won't change anything about your real identity. That's not who you really are. Finding your power has nothing to do with having it given to you by your forefathers. It has everything to do with realizing that you've had it all along.

When you're younger, it's easy to imagine that older people have access to some kind of secret power.   There might even be some resentment because you believe that they're not sharing those secrets with you. You become powerful not because you are given power. You already have the magic. You might not know what you're capable of until you are forced to demonstrate it. That's okay. Your mom or dad do not have any secret teachings, but you might not experience the power of that role until you become a parent, yourself. There's no secret, so we can move forward in trust. It's not power that gets passed on. Instead, it is a realization that we're all in this together, that each person has a job to do.

The beauty of all this is that your job changes as you grow, if you let yourself be in process and honor the journey. You'll be called on to do different things, and learn different things, from different people along the way.   As long as you claim a spiritual inheritance, rather than a temporal one, those transitions won't turn your world upside-down.

DIETER:

We're all in this together. We owe each other our best, and we give each other the freedom to express it in our own way. We meet people where they are at, not where we want them to be. The lesson comes from stepping outside of ourselves. Yes, you have to deal with your family. But they have to deal with you, too, so make some noise.

Your tribe may have been doing the same things for a thousand years. Maybe they're waiting for a hero who can show them a deeper love, a more profound insight, a bigger concept of service. Maybe they're waiting for you.

QUESTION HELPS

1. Why did you choose your family?
2. How do you define your family? If service is an element of your definition, what do you serve?
3. If your True nature is spiritual more than physical, what do you truly inherit, and where does it come from?
4. How has your role in your family changed over time? How can you honor the place you're in?
5. What's the best way to model the change your family is ready for?

CHAPTER SIX: WORK

Work does not have to be a four-letter word. Action, when combined with loving intention, is the key to a happy life and a peaceful world.

SEE:

Know that you have a deliberate purpose and a definite reason for being here; you have a divine gift. Your calling is calling you in and through every moment of experience.

SPEAK:

Instead of responding to outer conditions, follow your inner guidance and take your passion into action.

SURRENDER:

The universe takes care of its own. Trust the journey; it can only lead to prosperity.

DIETER:

Spirituality is more than what a person does on Sunday morning. Love is not just what you do when you're on a date. Learning isn't just for school. A big part of this journey has to do with breaking down boundaries. Put another way, living this life to the fullest means living it consciously, all the time. So what are we doing with that time? We spend a third of our lives, half of our waking lives, at work. For a lot of folks, work and identity are one and the same thing. More than that, most people don't look at work as something they have a choice about at all. It's an obligation. And that means that who they are is obligatory, when the desire to live deliberately is inherent.

Let's approach this from a place of consciousness, though. Let's ask. Why do we spend so much time doing what we do?

JENNY:

The obvious answer is that we have to do something that pays the bills. I think that's what most people would say. We need a place to live and food to eat. As always though, we want to go a little deeper with our understanding. You are more than your location or what you consume. I think the first step in figuring this out is to remember that our time is precious. Yes, you are an infinite being, but there is only right *now*. This moment of intention and attention creates your next experience. Cumulatively, that builds the world that we live in. Every moment is creative, so every moment is work.

DIETER:

There isn't anything wrong with that. In fact, work is the only way healing, or revolution, or growth can happen. Spirit doesn't happen to us. We are not supposed to sit around waiting for rescue or salvation. It happens through us. We play a part in the manifestation of Truth.

There is a precedent for work in Scripture, and work itself is never referred to as a bad thing. It comes up over and over again: "My Father is still working, and I also am working" (John 5:17), "So faith by itself, if it has no works, is dead" (James 2:17), "We must each work out our own salvation" (Philippians 2:12). Those quotes are just scratching the surface. Let's decouple the word work and the word toil, for example. The fact that work comes up so frequently, and in such a natural and good way, is instructive. Maybe we need to look at it as a positive; as part of our spiritual growth. Work is how we express our divine nature. Work itself is not a bad thing. The positives or negatives come not from work itself, but rather from our working consciousness. The question is *what* we choose to work on.

JENNY:

I would like to see a shift in the paradigm about how we see work. Work is absolutely part of our nature. There's a reason that it feels good to put in a hard day's effort. There is honor and pride there. A sense of accomplishment. That feeling usually happens with work or hobbies that we love. In those cases, the motivation comes from within. We tend not to get that good feeling from externally-motivated pursuits. In those cases, we feel forced, and the joy is gone. When the joy is gone, the productivity decreases, as well.

Whether the external factor is a person, a tradition, an obligation, or just money itself, we never get the same feeling we do when we work from inside-out. When we spend our time with passion, we move from surviving to thriving. What if every time we went to work we remembered that we don't buy things with money; we purchase them with time?

DIETER:

Part of this has to do with recognizing that all your time is worthwhile. You are always a divine being, so every moment deserves your divine best. You are not supposed to save your best self for certain times or audiences. The division between good time and bad time is a human construct. It might seem to make things easier to understand when we put them in terms of sections and opposites. That's completely artificial. The goal is oneness. Compartmentalization is the enemy here.

Some people have a problem with the word "religion," for example. There isn't anything wrong with the word, though. Spirituality is about how you feel, and religion is about what you do. We need both. It's good to want to do things. Religion is not the problem. In fact, it's often the solution. Feeling something on such a deep level and with such intensity that we take our passion into action is the name of the game.

The problem is not action. The problem is stagnation. More to the point, the problem is the behavioral transition between religion and life. As if the two were different things. If I save my divine self for certain people and places, I'm shortchanging a big part of who I am. I'm compromising my ability to make a difference in the world.   Ultimately, I'm hurting myself. Let's get to the point where we are the best version of ourselves all the time. Let's make life a religious pursuit.   We create our experience with our current thoughts, words, feelings, and actions.   If a third of the time we are thinking, speaking, and living in dread, the world we make isn't any fun.   Work is where we spend a bunch of our lives, and most people hate it.

JENNY:

They think they are *supposed* to hate it.   We trade miserable work situations like baseball cards. There are movies, songs, and shows about how bad work is and about how we are supposed to hate our bosses. What that tells us is there's plenty of negative material to work with.

DIETER:

That's a problem because we end up with a world populated with the miserable.   It's a deeper issue because people identify themselves by their jobs. When you meet somebody, right after they tell you their name, they almost always tell you their occupation. So if I am my job, and my job is a miserable, pointless pursuit, what's my identity?

JENNY:

Exactly. There's something really strange that happens when people spend so much time trying to get away from something that is part of who they think they are. Many people work so they can escape and have a vacation. There are still others who go on a vacation so that they can be more productive at work. This second view sounds good and it's progress and is perhaps better than the standard view. However, both of these paths work for "success" and money. Those are external motivators, and we know about those. If that's all you want then you're all set. I'd argue that once you got to the "goal" you'd be looking for something deeper. What if the work, as an out-picturing of something you are, rather than what you do, didn't require time-outs?

If there are no accidents, than wherever you go, you are required. There is something only you can do. That is your divine gift. If you're not doing it, you'll never prosper. On top of that, what you *are* doing may make you miserable, but it could be someone else's real purpose. By settling for work instead of calling, you're not just hurting yourself.

DIETER:

I used to work a pretty soul-crushing job. I'd sit in my car in the parking lot and psych myself up to go into the building every morning. I wasn't the only one who dreaded that morning march. I knew we all felt like losers; it was palpable. One morning, as I was doing that trudge, I saw that one of the cars in the parking lot had a "what if they gave a war and nobody came?" bumper sticker. The point of those stickers is that we have to agree on something like that. Wars are not fought by leaders, they are fought by soldiers. On some level a bunch of people have to agree with the conflict in order for it to go on. In that moment, it occurred to me that work as toil is something we have to agree on, too. It's groupthink. What if we stopped participating in that model? What if we refused to share in the delusion? What if they gave a corporation and nobody came? As you know, I quit that job pretty quickly after that.

JENNY:

It can feel hard to break away from these ideas. We as a society tend to look down on people who don't fit into the definition of success that we've been given. Stay-at-home moms, "creative types," and people who work with their hands don't fit the established norm. It's important to understand that this paradigm is always in flux. Material success is not as solid of a concept as it might seem. We've talked about this before. These standards are culturally and geographically mediated. If you fixate on the details, your definition of success varies wildly over time and distance.   When we operate on a material level, we are on shaky ground.   As always, the trick is seeing past the current temporary state into the permanent ideal.

DIETER:

That's new. For a long time now, we've been sold the notion that abstraction is good. Somebody told us that the goal is to sublimate, to put our dreams on hold.   We thought that we would eventually be rewarded for our silent acquiescence.   There's a supposed external, eventual reward, and we get it by keeping our hearts locked away. Our True nature is growth and motion, and the stagnation feels wrong. That's why folks hate their jobs.   It's not the thing they do, it's the lie they feel that they have to tell to do it.

More significantly, if you take away the things that make you human, like your passion and your dreams, you become less of a human being.   You become a human *resource*, no different than a stapler or a delivery truck. Job security actually decreases when you throw your humanity out the window. It's easy to replace a stapler. It's hard to replace a loving, committed heart.

JENNY:

Young people are told that they have to pay their dues. Of course there's plenty to learn, but that's the way it is in the middle of a journey as well as at the beginning. The idea that young people, who in some ways are more in touch with their dreams and their hearts, ought to stay quiet, is madness. Any industry, any occupation, benefits from having passionate dreamers in it. Let's encourage them. Let's build a world where this is valued. Let's value it in ourselves, too. Let's find the dreamers sleeping in our own hearts.

We're often told that sitting still leads to job security; exactly the opposite is the case. What we want is honesty and integrity. Even the smallest effort to be your True self can cause a chain reaction.

Any growth in this area can make a difference. We want to get to an honest place. Start by being honest where you are.

DIETER:

The rich life has very little to do with money. If you are a worrier, you'll worry in a private jet. Let that go and focus on what is important. Interestingly enough, though, if you let that go, and take away the power that money has over your life, that tends to lead to outer success, too.

You know poor people who are happy and rich people who are miserable. There's a disconnect between money and happiness. It's not about what you would buy if you won the lottery; it's about what you would do. What would you learn? Where would you go? Who would you set free? Beneath the various specifics, most people say that if they won the lottery they could stop worrying. But you can quit worrying for free. In fact, that's the only way it'll work.

Prosperity has a lot less to do with materiality and a lot more to do with releasing fear and expressing freedom.

JENNY:

If you want to prosper, what you're not allowed to do is hate your job. It's the old lesson: You get more of what you put out. Instead it starts with thanksgiving. All that resentment does is disrupt the learning cycle. It stalls you and keeps you from the place you want to be. Complaining actually makes you less likely to make a positive change, because the energy you might have spent on growth gets used up in words. Whining provides an escape valve exactly where we do not need one. It's better for that pressure to be used as the catalyst for change.

DIETER:

You want passion and honesty. We all do. No outer situation will give it to you, though. Remember that life is lived from inside-out. So let's try to find moments of passion and honesty where we are right now. It's okay if you're not where you want to be. It's okay if you're not fulfilling your calling in every nanosecond. Just start by seeing your job as part of the divine outworking, and trust in the growth that has to take place. The "God bless the child" song has to do with being faithful with what you have, so that you can build your capacity to receive, and do, more.

JENNY:

We start by finding things to spend our now on that are meaningful, inside and outside of work. Decide what you are worth. Imagine that what you do now is a channel for that worth to go out into the world. If you do that, you'll end up being a committed worker. You may find that your job gets easier. You may also find that your job isn't a good channel for the light and love that only you can offer. That's okay, too. It means that you are allowed to move on. More than that, it means that somebody else is supposed to be doing the job you are currently doing. You're in the way. In that case, you owe it to yourself, to that other person, and to the world to move on. Either way, you win.

QUESTION HELPS

1. How do you define work? Why do you do what you do?
2. If there were no external or eventual rewards, would you still work at your present job?
3. If money were no object, how would you spend your time?
4. Can you see your present vocation as an opportunity to learn about and express your True calling? What will you do, based on this vision?
5. How can you start to express your heart's calling, even if it's only for a few minutes each day?

CHAPTER SEVEN: COMMUNITY

Each of us is here to make a positive difference, to be a catalyst for healing. When we seize the opportunity to inspire, we are doing our jobs.

SEE:

Right here and now, God is.   Remember that everything True about God is True about you.

SPEAK:

Be the revolution the world is waiting for by living your Truth.   Inspire outer change by living from inner permanence.

SURRENDER:

Get out of the way.   The unstoppable love of Spirit moves through you and makes the way clear.

DIETER:

People come to us with questions. I'm sure that to the folks asking them, the questions seem unique. On one level, it's fair to say that different people are chewing on different things. Some people want to get their love lives figured out. Some people are working on some kind of healing opportunity. Some folks are trying to get a bead on how prosperity might work in real life. The details differ, to be sure.

On the other hand, we've spent a long time on the idea that details aren't important. Facts change, and we're looking for Truth. We've talked about getting to the idea behind the thing a dozen different ways now. There's a sense in which the questions are each unique. There's a deeper sense where there is only one question. Everybody wants to know how to bring a bigger sense of presence, power, connection to bear on the here and now. Everybody has the same yearning.

Maybe the universal question is "how do you change the world?" The question is valid and important for all kinds of reasons. There are lots of possible answers; different people see different reforms and revolutions necessary. Some people might start with education. Some might start with conflict. There's a spectrum of material responses, as history has shown. Behind any physical action or institution, the answer has to be something deeper. I think it starts with desire. How do you change the world? Start by wanting the revolution.

I know that in a lot of situations and cultures desire is thought of as a bad, worldly, human thing. But what revolution or change started without the desire for things to be better? Of course desire can be an ego thing, if there's ego in it. However, if we decide that our heart's yearnings come from an infinite place, we can start to uplift them and hear the voice of the divine calling. The trick is to start where we are, even if the desire feels like something small. It's connected to the most profound thing there is, and we'll get stronger through the participation.

JENNY:

Real change starts with honesty. If you can be a clear channel for the desire you feel in your heart, and get things like ego out of the way, you have started your journey. Being honest with yourself will inspire you to be honest with those around you. We talk to our kids a lot about identity and authenticity. Identity is the signs you carry. It's who you claim to be. Authenticity is how well you live up to those declarations. If I say that I'm a vegetarian and you catch me eating a hotdog, I'm not being authentic. This is the case about every choice we have. We need both. The world needs both. Part of our job description is to tell our story to the world. The other part is to live up to that unfolding story to the best of our abilities.

Nobody is alone on this journey, as we've discussed. You are allowed to ask for assistance. It may sound odd but asking for help is a grownup thing to do. Being secure enough to say "I am

145

teachable" is mature.   Knowing that *not* knowing something doesn't make or break you, because your self-esteem is rooted in a deeper place, is the beginning of real maturity.   Show me someone who has to do everything themselves and I'll show you a three year old.   Everyone has heard a toddler holler "Me do it!"

DIETER:

Another important step is to remember that everything is a choice, even if it doesn't always feel that way. Some folks say that bad things are "the way of the world."   But the world, when left alone, is growth, order, and, when you look at it, love.   Put another way, the "world" is just made out of people like you and me.   Everything is the result of prevailing consciousness.   Every thought, word, action, expectation is a vote for the kind of world we want, and majority rules.

Life is the product of our choices.   Life is also what we choose to put up with.   There is no prize for enduring hardship for its own sake, or for putting up with a lie. Looking at history, monstrous things didn't happen because every participant was a monster. In most cases, the majority of people just didn't know how to stand up, or didn't think they could. Let's take the choice back. Bad things can happen otherwise.

JENNY:

Taking your power back takes courage, though. Fear is the problem. Some people have a real fear of being wrong. There's a fear of not being heard, or of being heard but not understood. There's a fear of not being loved or respected. It might feel hard to stand up for love, when there's a fear of separation. On the other hand, fear *is* the separation. Ultimately, we are all one, and the only thing that makes us feel alone and apart is fear. It's an illusion. You can't really ever be separate in spirit.

DIETER:

Let's go back to that formula we had at the beginning; it was the one that set us apart. We can turn it around and find unity. Just as you said a while back, you are enough. The world is good. You have access to the answers. Your thoughts and feelings can guide you in healing ways. That means you are good in potential and in expression.

JENNY:

We can apply this formula to every aspect of our lives. We've covered the topics of Self, Relationships, Family, and Work. As we talked about how to decode each of these roles that we play in life we discovered that there's a pattern. We work from inside-out, and that direction is expressed by inspiring an increasingly large group of people. Peace on Earth begins with the individual and expands outwards. We each may have small things to fix in one area and big things to overcome in another. Either way, the healing can happen, and it starts with consciousness.

DIETER:

We are really talking about the same thing, manifested in different ways. We are talking about love. If you understand love, you get all of this. We are talking about finding the one presence and power that unites the immanent and the transcendent, the facts and the Truth, the individual and the whole. That's love. Seeing ourselves, all others, and the world with those eyes is the beginning of revolution.

JENNY:

If love is the Truth, and the goal is to have our actions match that awareness, the way to change is to realize that the essential nature of all things is unchangeable and good. To bring that essence to the surface, we can't force it. We have to let it.

DIETER:

Exactly. I think there's too much emphasis placed on trying to make something happen or change something in the outer. Thinking that way ends up being dualistic. There's the action and the reaction, the pusher and the pushed, the force and the object. That can never get us to a place of oneness. The goal is not to make something happen, but instead to *be* something True. This is the path of love and unity. You know that quote that some folks have as their email signature, the "be the change you wish to see in the world" quote. Turns out Ghandi didn't say it, but it is still meaningful. It is easy to find statements along those lines, like Saint Teresa's "God has no hands but yours." The idea here is to feel the transcendent and model it. With that in mind, the only real adversary is waiting. Holding still affirms the wrong thing; something we don't want. If I'm waiting for spirit, my expectation is that spirit is not here, and it's hard to grow with that consciousness of absence at the core of my efforts. It's not about waiting for change. It's about being the change. It's not something that begins with what you do. It starts with what you know, what you feel.

JENNY:

Coming from that kind of place shines through everything we do. When we resolve to show the world what love looks like, real change happens. If you really believe that people are inherently good, you don't want or need to change them. We have to move from a conversion model to an inspiration model. We want to demonstrate and inspire.

What can you do to behold the good in somebody else? What can you do to show them the Truth about you? Think about how different that is than the old idea of trying to make people something different than what they already are.

DIETER:

As always, the refrain here is to get past the thing and into the idea. There is no power in things, the power is in love. So what do you love? To get there we might have to do some archaeology in order to figure out what it is that we really want. If you look closely enough, you inevitably see the face of the Divine staring back at you.

JENNY:

You are dynamic; you get bored. We have to move. We have to grow. There's a still small voice inside us all that's crying out. It's our job to answer the call. We can do this by building the habits that we want to see more of in our lives. Like you said earlier, start small; start where you are. Go after whatever it is with an open mind and heart, and you will grow.

DIETER:

Success has nothing to do with possessions or credentials. It has to do with with what we live. Jesus had no building, no diploma, nothing but the power of His Truth. That's my favorite story, but there are others, to be sure. And they all have conviction at their core.

JENNY:

You have what the world wants. As corny as it sounds, you are here to make the world a better place. You are the revolution. We all are. I believe in the goodness of humanity and our ability to create an extraordinary world. God is good. You are good. Go do good.

QUESTION HELPS

1. How do we change the world? What needs to change, if love is the Truth?
2. Where does change start, and how is it expressed?
3. What can you do to behold the good in somebody else? What can you do to show them the Truth about you?
4. What is the difference between conversion and inspiration? What is the goal?
5. Why are you here? How can you demonstrate your purpose?

CONCLUSION

Thank you for going on this journey with us. It has been a long trip, over a short period of time. In the nine months since we first put pen to paper, we have seen amazing and unexpected changes. We've had healing in our family, we've said goodbye to longtime friends. We left one church and started working at another. We've seen some incredible changes in our work and financial situation. All along, we've redoubled our commitment to the ideas we've been talking about. We've lived these principles to the best of our abilities, and have grown in surprising and beautiful ways.

It has been, and will always be, the case that we are not in charge of what happens next. That's been the biggest growth point of them all. Our job is to do our utmost, to work hard and in love, in peace and on purpose. We are not in charge, though. Over and over again, we've seen that we are neither the source nor the destination of the good in our lives. Moving out of the driver's seat has left us open to bigger ideas and unexpected profound experiences. Life has handed us phenomenal learning opportunities. We've done our best to take what comes, branch in and find the Truth behind the facts. When we do it, life gets easier. We grow.

This works for us. It will work for you, too. There is nothing special about us, in that we all partake in the same birthright. There's no special dispensation here. As with all areas of life, you get out what you put in. You get what you bring. We've given ourselves, all the treasures of our minds, hearts, and hands, to this life, and we are paid back a million times over every day.

You've been reading and thinking along with us. We bet you've already got some stories about how things have shifted. How have you grown? Has the universe asked you if you mean what you say? What's next?

There is always something next. But you know that already. You're on the path. Each moment, life calls to you in countless ways. The one infinite presence shows up in a million disguises. We are all here to see past temporal experience and into transcendent Truth. When we can see it, when we let that vision become a thought so powerful that it moves into feeling, a feeling so profound that it becomes an action, things change. Most importantly, we get out of the way and celebrate a new experience of what has always existed. We see, we speak, and we surrender.

Then we do it again. The beautiful spiral of life keeps on going. A consciousness of good brings about a good experience, which makes it easier to see the good the next time around. That's the job description. Even when our situation doesn't feel positive, our role is to find the love, the Truth, the triumph hiding beneath the surface and follow where it leads. Even the most negative emotions are worth praising, because they can tell us what not to do. Feel your feelings; the affirmative ones let you know you're on the right track, and the negative ones show you where you've been putting up with something hurtful. Either way, we are here to learn. We are here to do something with the gifts we're given.

In some ways, you're nearing the end of one cycle, but you're also at the beginning of a deeper journey. We encourage you to look back through the book.   Think about how you might answer the questions differently the second time around. What has stayed the same, and in what way? What have you released?   As you reflect on what you've outgrown and what you've focused on, you can do a little branching in on yourself. It's time to uncover the beautiful, triumphant, uniting Truth about you. The world wants what you have to offer.

The next step is sharing. As with every hero's story, your journey deepens and intensifies when you share what you've learned with somebody else. The fact that you picked up this book says something about you. The fact that, in so doing, you've made room for change, says even more. With that moment of intention for growth and attention to your heart, things have begun to shift for you. What can you do to keep that momentum going? What can you do to show the world what love looks like?

Please let us know how things are working for you. We're easy to find on the internet at UnitySociety.com or in person at one of our workshops. In the meantime, we're cheering you on, and we can't wait to see what happens next.

All One, Jenny and Dieter

ABOUT THE AUTHORS

We are Dieter and Jenny Randolph. We are here to remind you that God is Good, which means that you are good. When you know that, its your job to do good in the world. We started The Unity Society as a way to inspire this kind of life, but it's only one step in a long journey. The book you're holding is part of that trip.

We met when we were teenagers, and haven't left each other's side since. Along the way we've had amazing adventures and life-altering learning opportunities. We are still growing up together, and love sharing what we find along the way. In the course of a single year, we got married, started a storefront church, and saw the birth of our first child, all before either of us was old enough to rent a car. In the more than twenty years since then, we haven't stopped moving.

JENNY RANDOLPH

Jenny has always been a teacher. When she was still in high school she spent a summer teaching basic music to elementary aged kids. She and Dieter homeschooled their two children, Miles and Raina. As a result, Raina started college courses at the age of 13, and Miles at 15. The kids are all grown up now, and usually have something new to teach their parents. Jenny is a sponsor for the teen group at her home church; the same group where she met Dieter. In her capacity as sponsor, Jenny's been creating and running spiritual retreats for more than a decade. Jenny grew up on a Wyoming ranch, surrounded by horses, chickens, rabbits, cats, dogs and even a few horny toads as her pets. It was here that she learned to love all animals and has been a vegetarian for more than 20 years. She also learned the value of hard work and the joy of making things with her own hands. She does this in the kitchen by making her own bread, canning fruits and veggies and serving up some awesome vegetarian comfort food. Outside the kitchen there are always home repairs, upgrades, or art projects going on at the Randolphs' place. Jenny is fiercely independent and doesn't believe there's anything that can't be learned or fixed with a little moxie and hard work. She is here to live a fully awake and passionate life and hopes she can help you do the same.

DIETER RANDOLPH

A third-generation minister, Dieter has been on this path since childhood. He was born in Kansas City, Missouri, where his parents were studying and working at Unity Village. As a teen, he served in many leadership roles within the Youth of Unity, and it was in the Y.O.U. that he met Jenny. Throughout his journey, Dieter has been on fire about finding ways to take spiritual ideas beyond the traditional church setting. As he puts it, "I think that for something to be truly meaningful, it has to apply to everybody, not just people in one specific situation or community." With that idea in mind, Dieter has spoken and taught in countless venues and formats. Wherever he finds himself, people find him. Invariably folks come to Dieter with a hunger to grow, to find passion, to live deliberately.

Dieter is here to help you find a life that you love, one that feeds you instead of making you feel tired. We're all in this together. When you win, so does the world.

You can catch up with us by visiting our website, UnitySociety.com. You're going to love it.

www.ingramcontent.com/pod-product-compliance
Lightning Source LLC
Chambersburg PA
CBHW061823040426
42447CB00012B/2794